decorating with
color and texture

ROCKPORT

ROCKPORT PUBLISHERS

decorating with
color and texture

Ann McArdle

First published in the United States of America by
Rockport Publishers, Inc.
33 Commercial Street
Gloucester, Massachusetts 01930-5089
Telephone: (978) 282-9590
Facsimile: (978) 283-2742
www.rockpub.com

ISBN 1-56496-702-6
10 9 8 7 6 5 4 3 2 1

Design: Francesco Jost
Front cover images from left to right:

Fujiwo Ishimoto
courtesy of Marimekko

Matteo Manduzio
courtesy of Zimmer + Rohde
Zimmersmühlenweg 14-18
D-61440 Oberursel, Germany
Telephone: 06171-632-146
Fax: 06171-632-244

Back cover images:

Matteo Manduzio
courtesy of Zimmer + Rohde
Zimmersmühlenweg 14-18
D-61440 Oberursel, Germany
Telephone: 06171-632-146
Fax: 06171-632-244

Printed in China.

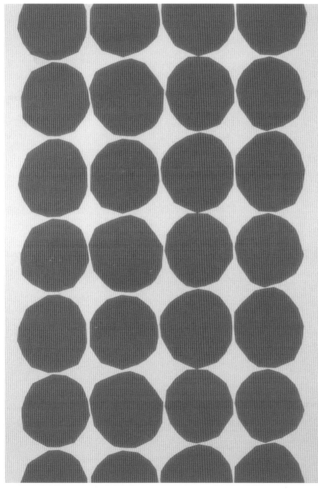

[ABOVE AND OPPOSITE]
Photos: Courtesy of Marimekko
Design: Maija Isola

Color is a tricky and sometimes subtle design element. That became obvious to me when I redid my kitchen. I wanted the walls to warm the white cabinets yet maintain the clean look of white to open up the small room and offset the dark granite countertops and oak floor. I wanted a white that picked up just a hint of the orange flecks in the granite countertops. With one corner painted the chosen color, I was horrified to see that, illuminated by the bright morning sun, the wall looked very much like a pink plastic Band-Aid. I cut the percentage of orange way down to achieve the look I was after. Now, at first glance, the walls appear to be the same color as the cabinets. But they're not the same; the orange tint in the white warms the room even though it is barely noticeable. Magic! I learned two valuable lessons from this experience: One, paint a test patch before you paint the whole room; and two, color—even when barely perceptible—can have a profound impact on the way a room feels.

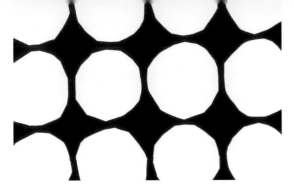

Texture has a similarly profound effect. The color we perceive is actually light reflecting off of a surface, and texture governs the absorption or reflection of light—thus affecting our color perception. For example, a wall painted yellow in a glossy finish will dazzle and energize, whereas the same yellow in linen will be slightly muted and less vibrant. Color and texture, then, become inseparable in their application.

Color's magic is not limited to painted walls. The fabrics and finishes you choose can bolster or defeat your intentions. A romantic bedroom can feel even more so when soothing colors are used in sensuous textures. Sleek surfaces give a monochromatic room a clean, almost austere look, but soft sculptured upholstery or rough, light-absorbing materials in a monochromatic room create a warm, welcoming feel.

In *Decorating with Color and Texture*, photos of various interiors by top international designers help you appreciate the roles of color and texture in interior decoration, and helpful hints teach you how to use color and texture to achieve the look you're after.

For a dramatic look, go for stark contrasts. Pair bold complementary colors to enliven your home, or use more subtle color variations and let a rich variety of textures create the impact.

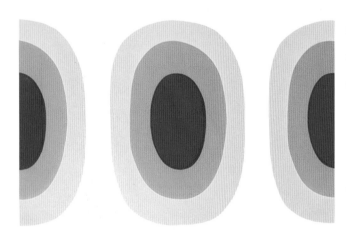

[ABOVE AND OPPOSITE]
Photos: Courtesy of Marimekko
Design: Maija Isola

If you want to adhere to a specific decorating style, enhance the look with colors and textures associated with that style. For example, you can give a contemporary room an up-to-date look with burnished fabrics, shiny metals, glass, and light-reflecting materials; for a taste of the Orient, include Chinese red in your palette.

For a unique look, express your own style with eclectic combinations. Transform a collection of disparate furnishings into a harmonious room with colors and textures that draw them together. If your furnishings already have a common theme, introduce an eclectic element by varying colors and textures in surprising ways—add bamboo side tables in a room with polished wood accents, let the sheen of brightly colored satin pillows spark a rustic room with a natural palette.

To focus on the way your rooms feel, choose colors and textures for the moods

they create. Soft, muted blue, green, and
neutral tones promote relaxation and ease;
yellows and reds energize and excite,
fostering lively conversation or a buzz of
activity. You can vary the effect with shades
or tints and textures that either enhance or
play down the overall scheme.

With the right colors and textures, you can
link your interior to the natural world and
capture the rejuvenating effects of a walk in
the woods or a day in the country as you
relax at home. Stone surfaces, cotton fibers,
unpainted wood, earthy tones, and natural
hues can give your rooms a fresh-air feel.

When you are aware of the magical effects
of color and various textures on color,
you can create a décor that both fits
your home and reflects your own style.
Your rooms will not only look right, they'll
feel right.

[OPPOSITE]
The color wheel keeps order among seemingly infinite possibilities of color choices. Use it to help you see the effects of mixed colors, to guide you in combining colors, and to keep you on track as you add elements to your décor.

Dramatic Contrasts

If you have had enough of the reserved look of monochromatic color schemes, create an exciting interior with dramatic contrasts of colors and textures. Play with contrasting colors in a bold palette to turn your home into dazzling space that energizes and invigorates. Or, maintain a soothing look, but add sensation with a variety of textures that set off an understated color scheme.

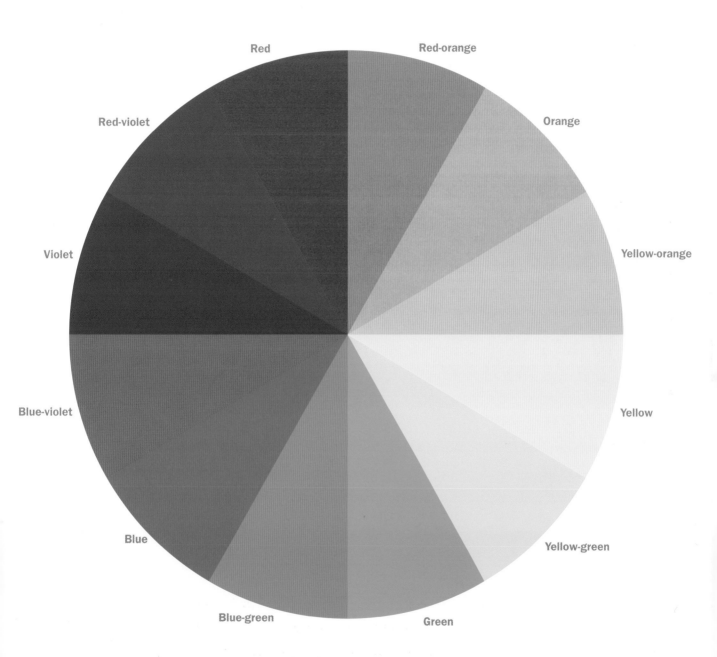

Red

Red-orange

Orange

Yellow-orange

Yellow

Yellow-green

Green

Blue-green

Blue

Blue-violet

Violet

Red-violet

Use complementary colors in large doses. You can create a lively look by juxtaposing a citrus green wall and one of coral pink, or choose less vivid colors for a more soothing, yet similarly dramatic effect.

Let the architecture of your home inspire color treatment. In a contemporary home, capitalize on the interplay of structural planes. An open staircase in a towering central hallway can be highlighted with color treatment. Paint one or two of the surfaces in a bright, saturated tone to emphasize the architecture and add excitement to the overall space. In a traditional building, an open staircase on an interior wall can become a design element if you paint stair treads in a color that echoes the world outside the door—shimmering blue for a waterfront spot, or a deep rich orange of autumn foliage. Transform a passageway into a frame with painted walls and ceiling in a lively color that offsets the rooms at either end.

Keep a few basics in mind when planning your colors. Complementary colors tame each other when mixed together and invigorate each other when side by side.

[OPPOSITE]
Accentuate architectural interest with color. Paint walls different colors to give an open space warmth and style.
Photo: Tim Street-Porter
Design: Frank Fitzpatrick

[ABOVE]
Optimize an archway as a frame for a view into other rooms. Surprising color in a complementary tone brightens and defines as it adds zest to the whole space.
Photo: Toshi Yoshimi
Design: J. Frank Fitzgibbons

[LEFT]
Use bright rectangles of color to define spaces in an open floor plan and make a small space impressive.
Photo: Paul Warchol, courtesy of B&B Italia
Design: Stamberg Aferiat Architecture for B&B Italia

Use the same color values when experimenting with contrasting wall colors or the result will be disconcerting rather than inviting. The more natural light your interior gets, the more comfortable and cohesive brighter colors will make your room feel. A room bathed in natural light is a better candidate for vibrant colors than one with limited daylight. Satin finish reflects more light than a matte finish. Augment the reflective effect with cut-glass or stainless steel accessories. Alternatively, use a metallic glaze over saturated wall color for a reflective benefit.

Don't neglect the natural wood in your interior when choosing your color palette. Polished mahogany creates a completely different aura than unfinished oak does. The difference is not only in the color but also in the light reflection. Include exposed floors, beams, and natural wood trim in your assessment of colors and intensities. If ignored, they can foil your plan by adding a color or color value that clashes with your scheme.

[ABOVE]
Make sense of a mass of planes and curves with dramatic color. A shocking chartreuse wall leads the eye up a winding staircase.
Photo: Toshi Yoshimi
Design: J. Frank Fitzgibbons

[RIGHT]
**An interior wall of brilliant red glass
adds vibrant color and high gloss to
offset cool concrete surfaces. A
spare sofa upholstered in a plush
chartreuse fabric provides textural
warmth and colorful counterpoint.**
Photo: Richard Waite
Design: Moutarde

Wall treatment alone can be the source of excitement, or take a less drastic approach and mix colors in your furnishings and accents. And don't limit your choices to the use of complementary colors. A range of analogous colors can provide drama while a variety of surface textures adds excitement.

- In a small powder room, paint walls a bold saturated color and furnish with shiny lacquered accents.
- Paint walls in a many-coated color wash in a rich plum tone, and upholster furnishings in woven fabrics of a slightly different tone, more red than blue.
- Add gilt accents to expand the richness of a color scheme and add dazzle to the light-absorbing fabrics.

If you choose a neutral tone for walls and floors, add dramatic color and textural interest with your furnishings. An unobtrusive backdrop recedes as chairs upholstered in a bold mix of bright colors fill the room with vibrancy.

- Cover chairs in shocking pink to enliven a casual sitting space decorated in neutral tones and natural wood.
- Use bold purple accent pieces to jazz up a pale yellow room.

[OPPOSITE]
Create a dramatic bedroom without sacrificing a restful ambience with violet walls to contrast with stark white flooring and accessories. Shocking pink shams add the vibrant note that gives this room life.
Photo: Courtesy of IPC Magazines Ltd.

[ABOVE]
Get a vibrant start to each day: In the bedroom, paint one wall sunflower yellow to catch the morning light. A spread in rich, complimentary purple gives the room pizzazz, while grey carpeting and upholstered bed keep the bold colors from overwhelming.
Photo: Toshi Yoshimi
Design: J. Frank Fitzgibbons

• Introduce an upholstered piece in a ruddy earth tone to a white room with natural wood furnishings.

A mixture of textures in surprising combinations can have as dramatic an effect as a bold color scheme, profiting from the distinctive light-absorbing qualities and the tactile characteristics of differing materials in similar colors.

• Add visual interest to a bedroom decorated in a restful neutral palette by adding a mohair throw, gossamer curtains, and pillow shams in a mix of lace, linen, and gleaming satin.

• Use bamboo side tables with a jute rug and rattan accent chairs.

• In the kitchen, select stainless steel appliances to reflect light, adding glitter to cabinetry in unfinished wood.

• Install crystal chandeliers for sparkle in a room furnished with dense velvets and richly piled carpet.

• Add a lime green upholstered piece to enliven a cool, stony interior.

Play with color combinations. Pay attention to their relative values and the effects of texture on their intensity. You'll soon find the combinations that bring your home to life.

[ABOVE]
Create architectural interest by using intense colors in complementary tones. Where burnt umber meets teal, what was an ordinary doorway becomes a warm, exotic corner.
Photo: Peter Margonelli
Design: Benjamin Noriega-Ortiz

[OPPOSITE]
Brighten a library corner with a reading chair in lemon yellow leather. Its sleek lines complement the shelving, and its color draws together the array of book jackets. Distressed legs soften the smoothness of the leather.
Photo: © Bill Geddes, 1999
Design: Dakota Jackson

[OPPOSITE]
Add interest to a built-in flat-front storage unit by applying colorful wood stains in random pattern. This technique gives a room real flair.
Photo: Tim Street-Porter
Design: Mark Mack Architects

[ABOVE]
Old wood, new wood, white plaster walls, and a cotton rug make for a lovely natural ambience—add a burnished metal chair in chartreuse, and the simple scene becomes a lively tableau.
Photo: Sam Ogden
Design: Albert Righter and Tittman Architects, Inc.

Complement richly pigmented wall color with furnishings in a related hue to enhance its impact. Magenta upholstery gives a complex brown wall a warm glow.
Photo: Grey Crawford
Design: Kelly Wearstler

[ABOVE]
Experiment with bold color in a dressing area and lavatory. Rich garnet walls create an exotic ambience that is enhanced by lacquered black accents and dramatic bathroom fixtures.
Photo: Glen Cormier
Design: Charlotte Jensen

DECORATING TIP

COLOR GROUPS

- The primary colors are red, blue, and yellow.
- Secondary colors are a mix of equal parts of two primary colors. On the color wheel, secondary colors are situated between the two primaries that make them up—violet (red-blue), green (blue-yellow), orange (yellow-red).
- Tertiary colors are a mix of equal parts of a primary and a secondary color. These colors appear on either side of the secondary colors on the wheel, and are usually named by the colors that make them up—red-violet, yellow-green, etc. There are six of these.

[ABOVE]
Add a touch of bold color to give a white-on-white room a dramatically different look. A rich purple tablecloth transforms an understated room into an exciting space.
Photo: Jacques Dirand
Design: Frédéric Mechiche

[OPPOSITE]
Complementary colors make the boldest contrasts. Pair intense orange and blue tones for a wild interplay of warm and cool, stimulating and sedate.
Photo: Antoine Schramm
Design: Robert d'Ario

COMBINING COLORS

- Complementary colors appear opposite one another on the color wheel (e.g., red and green, purple and yellow).
- Analogous colors appear beside each other on the color wheel (e.g., red and red-orange, yellow and yellow-green and green).
- Triads or split complementary colors are those whose positions on the color wheel form an equilateral triangle (e.g., red, blue, and yellow; violet, orange, and green)

[ABOVE, LEFT AND RIGHT]
Temper deeply pigmented primary colors with black and white accents. Dazzling goldenrod yellow walls are elegant and infuse the room with an uplifting glow.
Photos: Guillaume de Laubier
Design: Christian Badin

[ABOVE]

Make a restful dayroom a more lively spot by adding shocking pink cushions that spark the natural wood furnishings. Use gentler colors for the larger pieces so the room retains its relaxed feel.

Photo:

www.davidduncanlivingston.com

[LEFT]
Use shiny black accents—in this case, headboard, platform, and pillows—to turn a neutral bedroom into exquisite space without detracting from the restful ambience.
Photo:
www.davidduncanlivingston.com

[ABOVE]
Combine distinctive textures to turn a bedroom into a sumptuous space. A burnished metal bed offsets the polished wood of the wall unit. Shimmery drapes, ribbed carpet, cotton bedding, and intense wall color all bring warmth and richness to this room.
Photo: Alec Hemer
Design: Stedila Design

[RIGHT]
Dark walls and white woodwork create an exotic backdrop for furnishings with an Eastern flair. Light-colored upholstery in natural fabrics and light carpeting highlight the natural wood furnishings and artifacts.
Photo:
www.davidduncanlivingston.com

decorating with color and texture

FINE-TUNE THE CONTRAST: INTENSITY

Use similar intensities in contrasting colors, or the effect will be unsettling. The eye becomes accustomed to seeing one level of intensity and has difficulty adjusting to a duller or brighter hue in the same space. Balanced intensities allow the eye to perceive the full impact of the color combination.

[OPPOSITE]

Add a twist to a complementary color scheme by using two tones of blue accented with white and orange. A darker blue lends a sedate feel to an otherwise brightly colored room.
Photo: Peter Aprahamian, courtesy of IPC Magazines Ltd

[ABOVE]

Add warmth and drama to a pale blue room by introducing complementary orange accents. You don't need much to create the effect, and a light touch allows the tranquility of the blue to dominate.
Photo: L. Pope, courtesy of IPC Magazines Ltd.

FINE-TUNE THE CONTRAST: PLACEMENT

Where light reflecting off a colored surface can mingle with light from a surface of a complementary color, the impact of both colors is lessened in the same way that graying reduces the intensity. Place complementary colors side by side to heighten their contrast.

[ABOVE]

Enrich an open floor plan with textural contrasts. Galvanized stamped-steel walls add depth and dazzle while maintaining an industrial look. A marble tabletop puts a polished finish on the space.
Photo: Norman McGrath
Design: Hardy Holzman Pfeiffer Associates

[OPPOSITE]

In an airy, open living room, upholster clean, contemporary furnishings in bright complementary colors to create a warm, energizing ambience.
Photo: Peter Aprahamian
Design: Malin Iovino

[RIGHT]

Take a cue from modern abstract paintings to develop an invigorating palette for upholstery in a clean, contemporary space. The rug beneath the dining table echoes the colors and links the cool industrial dining area to the glowing sitting space.
Photo: Henry Wilson, Interior Archives
Design: Mark Guard

[OPPOSITE]

For a soothing East-meets-West look, hang drapery in panels of fabric that imitates bamboo shades to allow gleaming bare wood floors to catch the light. Choose leather chairs and keep the space uncluttered, in the Japanese aesthetic.
Photo: Courtesy of Zimmer and Rohde

Spark Your Style

Certain colors and combinations of colors are linked in our minds to specific styles, and because color and texture are almost inseparable in interior decorating, we associate a material with them as well. For example, the sheen of blue brocade suggests an elegant style, whereas the gentle radiance of linen in the same blue points to a more casual look.

[ABOVE]
In a minimalist white room, install dark walnut shelving and accent paneling to add dimensional interest. White vinyl upholstery is the epitome of sleek, while colorful frosted glass tabletops keep the sitting area front and center.
Photo: David Joseph
Design: Cha and Innerhoffer
Architecture and Design

Bearing in mind these associations, you can use the colors and textures in your own home to enhance the style of your interior décor. Unfinished wood, wrought iron, and natural fibers in neutral tones suggest a rustic style. Sleek blonde wood, a soft palette of peach and green, brass fixtures, and beveled glass speak of Art Deco. Polished mahogany and classic Wedgwood blue, golden yellows, and rich greens in shiny brocade create a stately look along the lines of Louis IV or American Federalist style. And stainless steel, concrete, and glass bring industrial modern to mind.

The architecture of some homes dictates a certain style. A Tudor home might call for period furnishings in Elizabethan style, with a palette of subdued primary colors in rich velvets and brocades, and carved mahogany woodwork. In contrast, a contemporary house of steel and concrete construction suggests a clean minimalist treatment in modern colors and flinty textures.

Sometimes location suggests a style. A beachfront home in a warm climate could call for Mediterranean colors and sleek, cool surfaces to catch the natural light. A

[ABOVE]
Perk up a clean contemporary look with brightly colored upholstery on streamlined pieces. Glass tabletops blend with the rainbow of colors to keep the room airy and light.
Photo: Bill Rothschild
Design: Marc Klein

mountain retreat of wood construction prompts the colors of nature in homespun textures and rough-hewn wood.

But in most city apartments and suburban homes, design style emanates from the interior décor rather than the exterior structure or its locale. In such a home, you can create a look that suits your tastes and lifestyle. Carefully select colors and textures in character with the style you choose to create a stronger statement with greater impact.

Give architectural design elements added weight with colors and textures that distinguish them.

• Define a decorative stairway with contrasting wall color to accentuate its lines and give it presence.

• Highlight crown moldings and decorative trim with color to strengthen their impact. Paint them to contrast with the walls or let them be the link between intense wall color and a pale ceiling with a value halfway between the two.

• Make the fireplace a focal point. Match upholstery and carpet colors in rich wool to color-saturated tiles in the fireplace surround.

[ABOVE, TOP AND BOTTOM]
Use color to define architectural details. A lemon yellow background gives a contemporary built-in wall display added life. A pillar becomes a striking element when highlighted with a lively color, in keeping with the youthful contemporary decor.
Photos: Courtesy of Poliform

[ABOVE]

Return to the 1960s by infusing your living room with hot colors and glossy surfaces. Even when the orange and shocking pink are balanced with Noguchi paper lamps, light-colored bolsters, and a neutral side chair, the room is brilliant. Its whimsy is unmistakable with a wall of television art—that is, nine sets resting in separate niches.
Photo: Paul Warchol, courtesy of B&B Italia
Design: Stamberg Aferiat Architecture for B&B Italia

**Give your breakfast area a light,
contemporary feel. Pair a glass-
topped table and translucent chairs
with soft cotton curtains in watery
blue-greens.**
Photo: Courtesy of Marimekko
Design: Fujiwo Ishimoto

• Accentuate natural wood trim and exposed beams with light-colored walls for contrast and earthy tones in furnishings and accessories.

• Complement stony construction with coarse textures and earthy colors for tables and kitchen surfaces.

Without architectural touches to guide you, create the style you want and add the right combinations of colors and textures to make it sing.

• In a plain white room, get a "mod" look with contemporary furnishings in an array of bright colors and richly textured mohair upholstery.

• Create a Chinese theme with red walls and black lacquered furnishings.

• Give a neutral color scheme an East-meets-West feel with bamboo furnishings and Japanese-style porcelain and earthenware.

• Install custom shelving of polished natural wood for a stately backdrop for dark leather furnishings.

• Design an elegant space with gilt accents and rich jewel-toned fabrics.

[ABOVE]
Distinguish a dining alcove from a larger space with wall and ceiling color. Carpet in a complementary color of stronger intensity visually shifts the weight to the floor, thus maintaining the light feeling of the stylized, contemporary furnishings.
Photo: Peter Margonelli
Design: Benjamin Noriega-Ortiz

[ABOVE]

Transform an essentially black and white contemporary living room into an expressionist masterpiece. Paint one wall (or a column, as here) deep red and match it with a carpet to demarcate the sitting area.
Photo: Roland Beaufre
Design: Eric Caspers Ciborowski

• Add glass-topped side tables to lighten a multicolored array of contemporary furniture.

• Choose lively bright blue and yellow drapery and bedcovers to evoke the feeling of the French countryside.

Once you've decided on your style, think about the images it creates in your mind. Notice how colors and textures are applied in other interiors of the same style. Be mindful of the effects of light on the materials you choose. The style will be clearer and the look more complete when the colors and textures are in keeping with the character of your décor.

DECORATING TIP

STYLE YOUR WALLS

Give painted walls a more complex color treatment or a textured look using one of these techniques:

• Colorwash—a mix of glaze and paint over a base coat of latex to create rich, multitoned effect

• Sponging—applying colors with sponge over a base coat to create textured effect

• Stippling—dabbing wet glaze coat (usually oil-based) with a dry brush to create a grainy texture

• Combing—dragging a comb across a wet base coat or glaze to create a wood-grained effect

[ABOVE]
Accentuate striking architectural elements with contrasting color reminiscent of their style. Here, the Islamic-style bookcase surround sets the tone for the room with its red finish.
Photo: Roland Beaufre
Design: Eric Caspers Ciborowski

**A dramatic fireplace mantel with a
mosque-like structure anchors the
decorating theme. It is shown off to
best advantage with walls of rich
vermilion and accessories of
stylistic line and simple colors.**
Photo: Jacques Dirand
Design: Patrice Nourissat

CREATE A HIERARCHY

Rank the surfaces in your room according to their importance. For example, if you have a wall with a fireplace that will be the focal point, rank that wall highest. The more important surfaces should have the warmest color treatments, which will make the surfaces stand out, accentuate their detail, or call attention to them.

[ABOVE]

Give a claw-footed tub an updated look with chili pepper red paint on its exterior. Repeating the color in tassel pulls on the shades finishes the look. In a roomy, uncluttered bathroom, the effect is magically lighthearted.

Photo: Simon Upton, Interior Archives
Design: Ruffle and Hook

A red wall is the perfect backdrop for Oriental treasures, Eastern-style pillows, and contemporary Western furnishings. Add natural wood and white cottons to keep the look fresh.
Photo: V. Welstead, courtesy of IPC Magazines Ltd.

MATCH COLOR TO STYLE

Neutral tones are restful and versatile. Sophisticated taupes and stony grays suggest an elegant interior. Pale terra cottas and sandy tones hint at rustic or casual settings. Choose the neutral palette that reinforces the style of your decor.

[OPPOSITE AND ABOVE]
Turn Eastern furniture into central pieces with a backdrop of colors and textures that speak of the Orient. Red walls enable a few treasures to project a total look.
Photos:
www.davidduncanlivingston.com

Add golden fringe to red velvet upholstered pieces to seal the classic look of a room paneled in luxurious, dark-stained wood.
Photo: Ken Rice

[OPPOSITE]
Give a room Eastern flair with Chinese red. For a lighter look, paper a faux wainscoting and match silk drapery to the wallpaper. Add rattan accents and silk kimonos to complete the look.
Photo: Courtesy of Nono

[OPPOSITE]
Use color and texture in the eastern
tradition to transform a room into
an exotic space. Simple accessories
in natural textures pair with
contrasting color of strong pigment
for an exotic look on a low budget.
Photo: Courtesy of IPC Magazines
Ltd.

[ABOVE, LEFT AND RIGHT]
Paint a small bedroom white and
allow the bedding to create the
style. Choose an energetic red floral
for a youthful, exuberant look or a
mix of fresh blue cottons for a
restful look.
Photos: Courtesy of Marimekko
Design: Kristina Isola and Fujiwo
Ishimoto

GET INSPIRATION FROM THE MASTERS

Look to major works of art for color inspiration. Observe the combinations in the works of van Gogh or Gauguin and use them for a lively look, or go for the softer combinations used by the impressionists Manet and Monet. The art of Delacroix and Géricault provide inspiration for a more bohemian color scheme.

[ABOVE]
Create an exotic Anglo-Raj look with textural interest. A cane headboard and a shiny black wood bed frame dress up a jute carpet and wicker baskets.
Photo: Mario Ruiz
Design: Mark Zeff

[ABOVE]
Turn a contemporary bedroom into a warm, welcoming room with soft cotton bedding, light-filtering sheer drapery, and a woven rug in the same neutral tones.
Photo: Courtesy of Zimmer and Rohde

Pair a plush gray sofa with light wood paneling for a soft yet masculine ambience in a sitting room. Muted tones and opposing textures form a restful spot.
Photo: Dan Forer
Design: Weixler, Peterson, and Luzi

Enhance an Art Deco look by setting off gray-blue furnishings with pink walls. Brass lamps, polished wood, and glass side tables complete the 1920s look.
Photo: Richard Richenbach
Design: David Webster and Associates

[ABOVE]
Nothing creates the atmosphere of a scholarly library better than dark wood and leather. Light walls and drapery and a tatami mat on a pale hardwood floor keep the dark elements from oppressing without losing their rich, solid quality.
Photo: Marianne Haas
Design: François Catroux

**Even contemporary spaces can have
a country feel. Decorate an armoire
in colors that match those in a folk
art wall hanging to achieve a sweet,
rustic look. A wicker chair adds
textural interest.**

Photo: Courtesy of the Iron Shop

[ABOVE]

**A fireplace surround of color-
saturated tiles can dictate the
character of your room. Deep blue
tiles with sunny yellow bursts give an
unmistakable Mexican flavor when
paired with terra-cotta hearth tiles.**

Photo: Ed Gohlich
Design: Maryclare Brandt

[RIGHT]
Use table settings to enhance a stylistic look. Earthy ceramic ware and natural accessories add the colors and textures of an eastern décor.
Photo:
www.davidduncanlivingston.com

MATCH TEXTURE TO STYLE

Choose upholstery fabrics and accessories in textures that enhance the style of your decor. A contemporary urban chic look calls for sleek leather, polished wood, and metal paired with metallic fabrics and silky satins. Light reflecting from these surfaces adds brilliance to the room. In a casual contemporary room, homespun fabrics and natural wood set a more relaxed tone. Their rough surfaces absorb more light, creating a softer, more serene atmosphere.

[ABOVE AND LEFT]
Highlight the architectural design of doors and windows with dark, medium, and light tones to delineate the detail. Warm taupe is an elegant backdrop for highly polished wood furnishings, giving even a small room an elegant look.
Photos: Eric A. Roth
Design: Robert Miklos

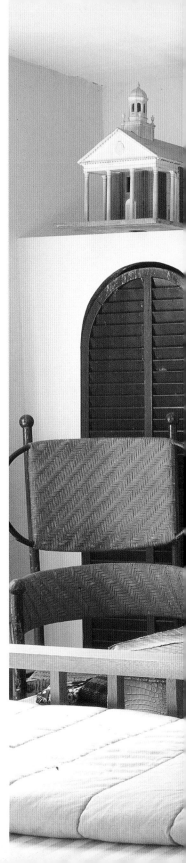

**Create an opulent look with a wild
mix of lustrous fabrics and rugged
surfaces. Rich autumn hues add to
the glitz with their warmth and
depth emphasizing the gold threads
in the fabrics and the metallic
accent paint.**
Photo: Dorothy Perry
Design: Tangee Harris-Pritchett

[RIGHT]
**Create a restful backdrop for rooms
alive with antique furnishings and
treasures. Silvery gray trim in a
flat finish is both quiet and
complementary to the aged wood
and plaster pieces. To lighten the
look, choose a satin finish for the
floor, and paint walls a paler gray.**
Photo: Eric Roth
Design: Richard Kazarian Antiques

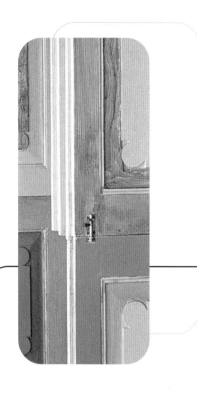

Eclectic Looks

Express your individuality by incorporating diverse styles into a comfortable, eclectic décor that brings together things that you love to create a look unique to your home. A successful eclectic look is a mix of styles, colors, and textures that blend into a distinctive yet cohesive whole. Use colors and textures to unite varied styles, or let them be the roots of the eclectic look.

Choose pieces because you love them, even if they represent different eras, parts of the world, or styles of living. Let their upholstery fabrics and materials build their association.

• Upholster a Queen Anne chair in an animal print to fit into a room filled with African drums and Native American leather pieces.

• Incorporate your grandmother's Mission-style chairs into a contemporary look with whimsically colorful seat upholstery to relax their weighty design.

• Link an ornate Old World chaise to a fresh, young decor with upholstery in a vibrant citrus tone.

Instead of focusing on the limitations of the furnishings you have, look on their differences as an opportunity to create a unique effect.

• Paint an odd collection of dining room chairs with red lacquer to whimsically tie them together.

• Arrange a grouping of like pieces (e.g., portraits, prints, or photos) and paint the wall behind them a saturated color to give it distinctive character.

• Link a mix of wood and rattan pieces with a jute rug underneath.

[OPPOSITE]
A soft pastel blue, cool but not icy, links large rattan pieces with sleek contemporary ones. Diaphanous white drapery and slipcovers on the dining chairs match the delicacy of the blue and equalize the heavy-to-light ratio to create a gracious room.
Photo: Peter Margonelli
Design: Benjamin Noriega-Ortiz

[ABOVE]
Turn a small kitchen into a happy corner with color to add interest and spark. Blue walls and colorful accessories brighten natural wood and stainless steel kitchen surfaces and tie into the artwork in the adjoining dining area, creating an exciting space.
Photo: Brady Architectural Photography
Design: Michael Borelli

• Transform a mix of furniture styles into an elegant seating area by choosing upholstery fabrics of similar sheen in rich gold tones.

Even though color and texture are the keys to uniting the assorted elements of an eclectic room, they can also be the source of variety and interest in a room with similar pieces.

• Set an elegant table in a casual dining area with a tablecloth of lustrous brocade in a richer shade of the wall color—deep green in a pale green room, vibrant purple in a cool blue room.

• Enliven a collection of white pillows with a mix of lace and linen, mohair and satin, corduroy and wool.

• Add surprise to a monochromatic natural palette with a gold satin pillow.

• Hang a gilt-framed mirror on a brick wall.

Transform a room from lackluster to exotic by mingling diverse colors and textures. Pair coarse with silky, matte with glossy for a texturally eclectic look.

• Hang shimmering drapery in the new metallic sheer fabrics to add spark to a contemporary interior rich in natural wood.

• Use brightly colored silk shantung for accent pillows in a counterpoint to concrete walls.

• Soften an exposed brick wall with sheer drapery that billows in the breeze.

[ABOVE]
Take color inspiration from an Oriental rug. The combinations are surprising in theory, but in practice, with the same color values, they can turn your room into a masterpiece.
Photo: Peter Margonelli
Design: Benjamin Noriega-Ortiz

[OPPOSITE]
In a light-filled open space, define functional areas with bright colors. Pair an orange kitchen wall with electric green dining chairs for an exuberant, eclectic look.
Photo: David Joseph
Design: Galia Solomonoff Projects

• Add satin pillows to a sofa upholstered in tailored wool.

• Pair leather chairs with a linen sofa.

Where artifacts and antiques are the eclectic elements, choose wall colors or furnishings in textures that add weight to their look and show them off to their best advantage.

• Add a metallic color wash over wall paint in a dark rust tone for a surprising glow that adds richness and depth to a room filled with earthenware and leather.

• Choose a neutral tone for walls and furnishings to offset a colorful display of treasures from around the world.

• Pair a rich wood Japanese tansu with streamlined Barcelona chairs in buttery leather.

A successful mix of eclectic furnishings, fixtures, colors, and textures is charmingly distinctive. Whether you're working with pieces you've collected over the years, setting out to buy everything new, or some combination of the two, you can indulge your eclectic tastes. Mix colors and textures to rejuvenate a tired look, or blend them to link diverse elements. The result will be a unique décor that bears your own personal stamp.

[OPPOSITE]
Let natural materials add a casual note to formal architecture. Bright area rugs show off hardwood floors, and lots of natural wood and cane furnishings tone down the high ceilings and decorative moldings that could make this room austere.
Photo: Roland Beaufre
Design: Eric Gizard

[ABOVE]
Fill an area with a sense of fun: Paint walls in color washes of varying hues to create a lively backdrop for a mix of styles in furnishings and accessories.
Photo: Paul Darling
Design: PGG Interiors

INCLUDE WOOD!

The wood surfaces in your room are part of its overall look, so make sure to include them in your plans. A room with exposed beams in yellow oak needs a palette that works well with the color of the wood. Polished mahogany paneling, on the other hand, calls for a completely different color scheme. Hardwood floors, natural trim, fireplace surrounds, and exposed stairways all must be considered when choosing your color palette.

[OPPOSITE]
Enhance the restful feel of a neutral palette with soft textural shifts that warm the space. Natural wood and leather add a weathered, comfortable note to an all-white room.
Photo and Design: Vicente Wolf

[ABOVE]
Two like sofas can become eclectic elements when upholstered in boldly contrasting fabrics. Vibrant complementary colors energize a neutral room.
Photo: E. Reeve, courtesy of IPC Magazines Ltd.

Set eclectic furnishings against bare hardwood floors and unadorned white walls. For a textural twist, juxtapose a raffia lampshade, gleaming glazed pottery, and pillows that look like balls of fluff.
Photo: Elizabeth Zeschin
Design: Carden Cunietti

CHOOSE CONTRASTING TEXTURES

Let the textures of upholstery and pillow fabrics create an eclectic look. Combine linens and brocades, chenille and satin, raw silk and organdy, chintz and muslin. Even if the color is the same, the way light reflects off the different surfaces will make each look distinctive.

[OPPOSITE]

Link the two main elements in this dining room: the textured heavy linen settee and the cool marble table. Mint green walls in an eggshell finish. Pillows in related greens help unite the space; the gold chair adds an elegant counterpoint.
Photo: Michael Dunne
Design: Laura Bohn

[ABOVE, LEFT AND RIGHT]

Doors can be the element that gives your room a distinctive look. Apply coordinating colors using various textural painting techniques to accentuate the details and individualize the space.
Photo: Charles Correa
Design: Charles Correa

Tame soaring ceilings and a rough-hewn post-and-beam structure with bright colors and lots of detail at eye level. Stone, brick, and unfinished wood become warm and welcoming when the textures of the outdoors are blended with the comfort of home.
Photo: Tim Soar
Design: McDowell and Benedetti

LOOK FOR UNIFYING COLOR

Pick a color from your assortment of treasures—a rust glint in earthenware, the yellow-brown of a bamboo table, blue-white from Chinese porcelain. Use this hue for walls to create a backdrop that enhances the presentation of an eclectic mix and calms its variety.

[ABOVE]
Transform an elegant sitting room with bold color in a mix of textures. Vibrant emerald green and animal prints add a surprising casual note to make a formal room more inviting.
Photo: Double Image
Design: Yoggy Crow, Inc.

[OPPOSITE]
In a successful eclectic room, everything is surprising, yet nothing surprises. A satiny brocade in deep green makes an elegant tablecloth in a casual room loaded with personality. Rustic chairs upholstered in a variety of fabrics add individual statements, and quiet green walls tame the space.
Photo: Guillaume de Laubier
Design: Michelle Halard

[OPPOSITE AND ABOVE]
Give your home a distinctive character with exotic artifacts. Delicate ceramics, natural wood, colorful woven carpets, shiny lacquered pieces, lush mohair, and wrought iron together create a fascinating display. Neutral walls provide a quiet backdrop, and a subtle tint in the trim adds dimension.
Photos:
www.davidduncanlivingston.com

CHOOSE AN ACCENT

When adding an accent as an element of surprise, don't hold back. Choose a texture that reflects light and a brilliant color that goes beyond your palette. Such a piece will be outstanding in a room where color intensities and values are similar and light-absorbing textures prevail.

[OPPOSITE]
Create a cozy dining corner near a window with a bright splash of yellow and a mix of styles and textures. A glass table allows visual room for a comfortable upholstered chair. Greenery from outside is reflected in the tabletop, giving a natural touch to a relaxed look.
Photo: Tim Street-Porter
Design: Annie Kelly

[ABOVE, LEFT AND RIGHT]
Mix colors and textures in surprising ways to electrify a corner. Or, to create a more refined look, let the textures speak for themselves in a less varied color scheme.
Photos: Ken Rice

[ABOVE]

Nudge your traditional bedroom into the twenty-first century while maintaining its character. Paint one wall a lively, bold color to accent the other walls and carpet of airy, light tones. Add an array of pillows in a mix of textures and colors to soften the contrast, lending harmony to the overall look.

Photo: Courtesy of IPC Magazines Ltd.

[OPPOSITE]

Give a room full of antiques a spirited look. Echo the colors of upholstered chairs in the window treatment and bedcover, but in a brighter intensity that gives the room a fresh look.

Photo: David Phelps
Design: Linda Chase

**Nestle a curvy upholstered bed into
a corner, all in stark white. The bed
is cloudlike with its array of pillows
in a mix of lace and cotton. The
golden tones and textural appeal
of a bamboo screen add a touch
of warmth.**
Photo and Design: Vicente Wolf

DECORATING TIP

ADD SPARKLE

Glass surfaces and crystal chandeliers can be effective means of adding a brilliant surprise to a room that lacks pizzazz. For the best results, position these pieces so that they catch both light and color reflected from another surface.

[ABOVE]
Pair delicate silk sheer drapery with natural elements of stone and hardwood for a surprising blend of plain and fancy. The look is restful, sleek, and contemporary.
Photo: Courtesy of Zimmer and Rohde

[RIGHT]
Turn a neutral bedroom into an elegant space with a lustrous gold satin bolster atop a textured cotton bedspread.
Photo: Matthew Millman
Design: Dianna Wong

To a restful neutral pallette, introduce textural interest to add dimension to the space. Pair gauzy white drapery with lush chenille and natural cotton bed coverings to offset the painted and natural wood surfaces for an exciting mix of delicate and rugged, plush and sleek.
Photo: Peter Margonelli
Design: Benjamin Noriega-Ortiz

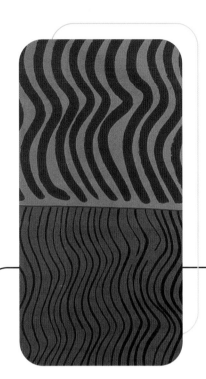

[OPPOSITE]

Dress your living room in summer white for refreshing relief from the scorching heat. A clean white screen blocks the sun, and a sofa covered in crisp cotton provides a cool resting spot.
Photo: S. Whitmore, courtesy of IPC Magazines Ltd.

Enhance Comfort

When it comes to making a house a home, comfort is as important as beauty—not just comfortable furniture, but comfortable rooms. Your home should *feel* right, so when you return at the end of a busy day, just being there is relaxing. With the right use of colors and textures, you can enhance the essence of your home by creating an ambience that fits your temperament and lifestyle.

**In a formal space with classic
architectural molding, you can create
a feeling of ease with color and
texture. Use crisp cotton upholstery
in pastels so pale they're almost
neutral. Paint walls with a grainy
texture and add a jute rug to further
relax the look.**
Photo: Guillaume de Laubier
Design: Christian Badin

Choose colors for the emotional impact they create. In their purest forms and simply stated, red enlivens and invigorates, blue calms, and yellow makes us happy. The secondary colors blend the attributes of the two colors that make them up. Orange (red and yellow) is invigorating and makes us happy, green (yellow and blue) uplifts and relaxes, and purple (blue and red) invigorates and calms. As colors become more complex, the effects of all the components commingle, tempering the responses they trigger. Similarly, when texture is added to the recipe, the effect is altered. How color is reflected affects our visual perception as well as our emotional reaction to it.

Of course, human response is never this straightforward. Personal preference and cultural experience can alter the effects of certain colors on you. Pay attention to your own reaction to colors. If you don't like yellow, for example, a room decorated in yellow will not make you happy, no matter what the books say.

Colors further affect the ambience of a room by projecting a sense of warmth or coolness. Reds, yellows, and their combinations are perceived as warm,

[ABOVE]
Sunny yellow walls ensure to a cheerful ambience. To keep the exuberance in check, gray the tone for furnishings and floors.
Photo: Tim Street-Porter
Design: Josh Schweitzer, Schweitzer BIM

[RIGHT]

Create a serene atmosphere to quiet your mind. Neutral tones—from white to jet black, in a mix of textures—in the upholstery convey a sense of calm when positioned among woods stained dove gray and deep brown.
Photo: Laura Rensen
Design: Thomas O'Brien

whereas blue, green, and violet are cooler colors. Be mindful of these attributes as you choose your color palette, but don't rule out cool colors if you want a warm room; instead, manipulate them with pigment and texture. For example, warm a room decorated in pale green by adding a yellow component, upholstering furniture in neutral-toned nubby wool rather than leather and choosing side tables in wood rather than glass-topped stainless steel.

The right colors and textures can create a mood, boost spirits, energize your work, relax your mind, or spark creativity. For a romantic room, try pastel colors and soft furnishings for a dreamy look and feel. Set a serene tone with neutral colors in soft wools and tweeds. Create a formal mood with elegant taupe walls, brocade upholstery, and highly polished wood furnishings. Project the buoyancy of your personality in a sunny yellow room. Let the deep, textured brown of hardwood floors set a quiet mood for reflection. Promote vitality by adding bright red to your palette.

Choose greens, blues, and neutrals to create an aura of calm. Use sleek surfaces if you want a cool feeling. For a tranquil spot

KNOW YOUR HUES

Colors are seen as warm or cool. The warm colors appear on the color wheel from yellow-green through violet. The cool colors are on the other half of the wheel—that is, from blue-violet through green. Warm colors are said to advance and cool colors recede. Therefore, a room painted in warm hues will seem smaller than if painted in cool ones.

[OPPOSITE AND ABOVE]
Warm gray exudes sophistication and poise. Neutral upholstery in a gently textured fabric soothes as it lightens the space, calming the aura of a richly appointed room.
Photos: Steve Vierra
Design: Marian Glasgow

[LEFT]
Paint walls minty green with an eggshell finish to provide a soothing ambience in the bathroom. Flat-front cabinets, sleek natural tiles, and a cashmere granite countertop add serenity.
Photo: Michael Dunne
Design: Laura Bohn

[LEFT]
Pale green and neutral tones induce relaxation in an airy living room. One wall painted brighter blue creates a focal point and adds dimension to the open loft space. Pillows in blues and greens link furnishings to the wall color and add cozy comfort in a spacious, uncluttered room.
Photo: Michael Dunne
Design: Laura Bohn

that will envelop you in comfort, choose warm wood and fabrics that invite touch.

• Paint a bathroom powder blue in a satin finish. With white fixtures, the look will be clean and sleek.

• Add velvet pillows in a leafy green to a sofa upholstered in neutral wool. The colors are even quieter in dense, cozy fabrics.

• Blue is especially suited to bedrooms. Warm it with a rosy tint and add a shaggy rug to delight bare feet.

Create a room that energizes and invigorates with reds and yellows.

• Ensure lively dinner conversation with rich ochre walls. They'll play with sunlight and glow by candlelight.

• Pile red mohair pillows on a denim sofa in the family room.

• Paint furnishings in bold primary colors in a satin finish for a lively children's room.

• Choose the palest yellow for a bedroom and quiet it with its complement, an equally pale violet, in bedding and drapery.

Use the characteristics of color to set the mood you want. With added textural impact, you can create a home that is comfortable as well as beautiful.

DECORATING TIP

PUT ANCIENT CHINESE WISDOM TO WORK FOR YOU

In feng shui, the ancient Chinese art of placement, colors are linked to the Five Elements (fire, earth, metal, water, and wood), which, in turn, are related to different aspects of our lives. The belief is that use of a color improves the flow of energy in the corresponding area, thus improving that aspect of our lives.

• Red: Fire—wealth, power
• Yellow: Earth—health, well-being
• White: Metal—children
• Black: Water—career, wisdom
• Green: Wood—family, life

[ABOVE]
Violet-red conveys a quiet, yet invigorating look. A rich velvet fabric contributes to the soothing effect.
Photo: Courtesy of Zimmer and Rohde

COLOR YOUR EMOTIONS

Colors have emotional impact. Red is energizing, yellow makes us happy, and blue promotes serenity. The secondary colors carry traits of both primaries that make them up. Thus, orange energizes and cheers, green uplifts and relaxes, and violet has a strong effect that combines excitement with ease. More complex colors have correspondingly complex combinations of effects. These effects can be tempered by tinting or graying.

[RIGHT]
Create a romantic atmosphere with lustrous fabrics in the colors of peaches and cream. Even a book-lined space becomes soft and alluring with such inviting hues.
Photo: Peter Margonelli
Design: Benjamin Noriega-Ortiz

[LEFT]
Convert a tranquil green dining room into a romantic fantasy with delicate china in pastel shades.
Photo: Roland Beaufre
Design: Madeleine Castaing

[LEFT]
Petal pink walls and wispy potted plants create a romantic feeling in a dining alcove. A fireplace surround in deep, rich tones keeps the room from looking overly feminine.
Photo: Bill Rothschild

[ABOVE]
A yellow entryway makes a warm welcome. A rich saffron shade is brightened by sunlight during the day and glows in artificial light.
Photo: Grey Crawford
Design: Jeffrey Alan Marks

SET A MOOD

Create an environment that sets a mood. Decorate a room to instigate fun with primary colors or bold secondary colors. Make sure to include colors with red and yellow for lively entertainment. For a tranquil spot that is meant to rejuvenate, use cooler colors—not too intense—in soft textures that will encourage the tensions of the day to melt away.

[ABOVE]

Start the day right in a breakfast room decorated in a palette of white and cornflower blue. Crisp cotton drapery and table linens make the space fresh and inviting.
Photo: Courtesy of Marimekko
Design: Kristina Isola and
Fujiwo Ishimoto

[ABOVE]

Just a touch of red at the breakfast table will get you off to a good start. Cotton drapery in an airy print with small red blossoms provides a boost of energy.
Photo: Courtesy of Marimekko
Design: Kristina Isola and
Fujiwo Ishimoto

[RIGHT]
Whether you prefer to cook in or eat out, you still have to spend time in the kitchen. So, give yourself a lift with colorful red-stained cabinets. Paint the walls and ceiling summer sky blue, complete with fluffy clouds, to add the serenity you'll need when the spaghetti boils over.
Photo: Ken Rice

[RIGHT]
Portray your sense of humor by pairing bold decorating colors with your whimsical collections. Primary colors in a mix of leather, velvet, and painted wood set a wacky, fun-loving mood.
Photo: Ken Rice

How do these three different color combinations make you feel? They all energize, but the pastel tones also calm, while the bold colors burst with vitality.
Photos: Courtesy of Marimekko
Design: Fujiwo Ishimoto and Kristina Isola

Primary colors work their magic in small doses. Bright trim and pillows enliven neutral walls and furnishings in a family room.
Photo: Courtesy of IKEA

decorating with color and texture

[OPPOSITE]
Give your dining room a party atmosphere with tableware, upholstered chairs, and wall hangings in bold primary colors and an assortment of textures— reflective glass, marble, blond wood, and lush velvet.
Photo: Peter Margonelli
Design: Marshall Watson Interiors
Ltd. and Adair Matthews

COLOR YOUR PAIN AWAY

Color therapists believe color can be useful in alleviating pain and illness through its vibrations. Use of a certain color can promote health in its corresponding body part.

• Violet—nervous system, brain

• Indigo—pituitary, ears, eyes, nose

• Blue—thyroid, throat

• Green—heart, lungs

• Yellow—pancreas, spleen, gallbladder

• Orange—reproductive system

• Red—kidneys

[ABOVE AND OPPOSITE]
Note your response to the colors in these fabrics. Does one feel more restful than the others? Is one more invigorating? Which is the warmest?
Photos: Courtesy of Marimekko
Design: Maija Isola

[ABOVE]
**Make your mornings happy with
perky yellow in the bedroom.
Balance pure, intense yellow with
an airy print in coordinating colors.**
Photo: Courtesy of Marimekko
Design: Kristina Isola

[ABOVE]
Use warm violet acccents to add a romantic touch to a bedroom of hushed blues and grays.
Photo: Van Den Berg
Design: Ravage

[TOP]

When choosing your colors, remember the emotional effects that they create: Red energizes, yellow is cheerful, and blue promotes a restful calm.
Photo: Courtesy of Marimekko
Design: Fujiwo Ishimoto

Soft dove gray and deep, rich wood stains create a calming look. Warm the slightly chilly walls with an animal skin rug.
Photo: Laura Rensen
Design: Thomas O'Brien

[OPPOSITE]
**Blend woven raffia sofas with rustic
pine and polished ash for a mix of
natural textures that emulates the
out-of-doors. Jolt the neutral palette
with delphinium blue accent pillows
in a sleek fabric.**
Photo: Michael Mundy
Design: Zina Glazebrook

Get a Natural Look

A breath of fresh air is a rare treat for those of us caught up in today's world of congested cities, underground transportation, air-conditioned automobiles and buildings, and Internet shopping from home. Experiencing nature becomes an activity in itself, often relegated to vacations. To reclaim some of the vitality that comes from being in the natural world, integrate it with your home by generating an outdoor feel with colors and textures reminiscent of the natural landscape.

You don't need rustic architecture or a country decor to achieve a sense of connection with nature; just use elements that, by their color or texture, remind you of the outdoors. Even the most elegant, highly polished mahogany table bears nature's stamp and, in the right surroundings, can be a hallmark of natural beauty.

Get inspiration from your favorite outdoor places. If you long for a sandy beach, choose neutral tones for large upholstered pieces in grainy cotton weave or raw silk, mimic the blue of the ocean in the wall color or carpet, and add accents of sunny yellow to complete the landscape. In a casual room, enhance the beachfront feel with rattan furniture and jute rugs. Drape windows with the airiest batiste to waft in the breeze, or choose bamboo shades that filter light without enclosing the space.

If a leafy glade is what invigorates you, choose a palette of greens and earthy brown in soft fabrics. For a light effect, choose linen or cotton; if you prefer to nestle deep in the woods, choose velvet or another nappy fabric. Incorporate stone surfaces into

[OPPOSITE]
On a screened porch, choose weathered furnishings to enhance the outdoor ambience and suggest a picnic in the woods.
Photo: Pieter Estersohn
Design: Berns Fry

[ABOVE]
Terra-cotta tile flooring sets an outdoor stage for an indoor dining area. Brighten natural wood and light walls with colorful accents to add a floral essence to the greenery outside and the stoneware within.
Photo: Atelier Wong
Design: Linda McCalla Interiors

the room—slate tabletops or a granite fireplace surround. Add potted plants and a tabletop fountain for total immersion in the atmosphere.

If a favorite room has a natural view, use it as inspiration for your decorating choices. Leave windows bare, but frame the view to make it the focal point. Natural wood is always suitable, but if your trim is painted, try deep forest green to frame a woodsy view, sandy white for an ocean view, sky blue or dove gray for a mountain view. Imitate the colors in your furniture and accessories to further integrate outside and in. With slipcovers, you can change the feeling of the room to reflect the changing seasonsæcool greens in airy cottons for summer, earthy tones in lush tapestry or chenille to match the autumn landscape.

If your view is not so inspiring, you can create a Japanese garden in a window bay with potted plants and smooth stones to represent woods and stream. In a room with natural wood, white or neutral tones paired with earthenware accessories create an effect that equals any view.

Without recreating a specific environment,

[ABOVE AND OPPOSITE]
Turn your porch into a jungle. Brick flooring makes plant watering less troublesome, so there's no such thing as too many potted plants. Exotic sculpture, bentwood chairs, and pillows covered in wild fabrics add to the atmosphere.
Photos: Tim Street-Porter
Design: Tony Duquette

[ABOVE]
Pale neutral tones, white, and natural wood create an airy outdoor feel. Bamboo shades filter light and let the silhouettes of trees outside form a surrealistic landscape.
Photo: Charles Correa
Design: Charles Correa

[OPPOSITE]
Heighten the airy natural feel of bamboo with accessories that imitate the texture and complement the form. Twiglike stands hold potted plants high, allowing the bamboo shade behind to frame the composition.
Photo:
www.davidduncanlivingston.com

you can make choices in your home that connect it with the outdoors in subtle ways.

• Choose natural wood for kitchen cabinets, or color them with a wood stain (rather than paint) so that the grain is visible. Pair them with granite or slate countertops—they're practical, beautiful to look at, and sing of the earth.

• Cover your duvet in natural cotton, and pile on pillows covered in cottons and linen. Paired with light-colored wood furnishings, they recall the freshness of a country morning, even in the midst of the city.

• Use slate and stone surfaces in bathrooms for their clean outdoor feel.

• On painted walls, use colorwash techniques to create a stony look with a range of grays and russets.

• Paint walls and trim in warm pastels that evoke the beauty of a desert sunset.

Optimize spaces in your home where outdoors and indoors meet. A porch affords you the convenience of home while you breathe in the fresh air. A three-season porch is a great place for small gatherings or a quiet read. Key the furnishings to the surroundings as well as the function of the room. If the porch overlooks a garden, you

decorating with color and texture

[ABOVE AND OPPOSITE]
Create a quiet sensation of harmony with nature with a neutral palette. The distinct texture of each element provides visual interest without disturbing the overall calm.

Photo: Andreas von Einsiedel
Design: Kelly Hoppen

Photo: Eric Morin
Design: Kelly Hoppen

might want white wicker chairs with cushions covered in soft fabrics in floral colors. A tree-lined view might inspire rustic wood furnishings. On an urban porch, you can create a garden atmosphere with a jungle of potted plants and comfy outdoor furniture to nestle in.

Let your love of nature guide you in choosing design elements that connect your home to the outside world. Use paint and fabrics, stone and wood to convey the feel of a revitalizing fresh-air retreat.

DECORATING TIP

CHANGE WITH THE SEASONS

Give your home a seasonal wardrobe! Use cotton slipcovers and lightweight curtains in white or cool pastels in summer. As the weather cools, remove the slipcovers to reveal upholstery in warmer colors and more light-absorbing fabrics. Add pillows in burnished autumn tones and a mohair throws for a cozy winter feel.

[RIGHT]
Shades of gray from black to white in rough concrete, polished wood, metal, and ceramicware form a restful ambience that offers visual quiet and tactile stimulation.
Photo: Richard Mandelkorn
Design: Celeste Cooper

[OPPOSITE]
Complement limestone flooring with a honed bluestone tabletop. Sisal and wood chairs add warmth and textural counterpoint, linking a sleek interior dining area with the outside world.
Photo: Paul Warchol
Design: Gabellini Associates

[ABOVE]
Leave hardwood floors bare and let wood trim serve as window treatment to achieve a natural look in the heart of the city. Leather, wood, and a screen reminiscent of outdoor fencing add to the earthy feel. White walls recede and let the warm elements work their magic.
Photo: Eduard Hueber
Design: Scott Marble and Karen Fairbanks Architects

[RIGHT]
Take advantage of the powerful presence of original wood flooring balanced with other fine wood details to achieve an overall natural warmth and ambience.
Photo: Paul Harmer
Design: MMM Architects

**Stone flooring and plain white walls
make a bathroom feel clean and
spare. A large tub and no-nonsense
washbasin add to the purity of the
ambience. Windows open to leafy
greenery outside seal the fresh look.**
Photo: Michael Mundy
Design: Zina Glazebrook

**Introduce natural elements to soften
the edges of an industrial-style space.
These lift-top chests in honey-toned
Douglas fir add utility as they warm
the bath surfaces of painted brick,
glass, and metal.**
Photo: Ed Reeve
Design: Adjaye and Russell

[OPPOSITE]

Use natural materials in warm earth tones to bring the spirit of the outdoors to a wide-open sitting area while emphasizing the comforts of warmth and shelter.
Photo: Rion Rizzo, Creative Sources
Design: James Edwin Choate, Surber Barber Choate, and Hertein Architects

[ABOVE]

Marry form and function in the kitchen with natural materials that are both beautiful and utilitarian. Limestone flooring sets a clean, restful tone, and cherry cabinets introduce wood grain and rich color to warm and soften the look.

Stainless steel appliances and countertops add vigorous shine.
Photo: David Joseph
Design: Cha and Innerhoffer Architecture and Design

CHOOSE YOUR NEUTRAL PALETTE

Get inspirations from nature for the neutrals that work for you. A collection of seashells offers a range of rosy hues and whites; a streambed can inspire variations of grays and browns; tree bark or a lichen-covered stone wall provides an array of grays, browns, and greens.

[ABOVE]
Get a fresh-air feeling indoors with crisp white slipcovers that show off natural elements: a hand-woven linen rug, a natural wood table, and straw and reed baskets.
Photo and Design: Vicente Wolf

[OPPOSITE]
In a room with a neutral palette, introduce a wide variety of textures that create depth and interest. Mix shiny marble with old wood, leather, and stone to capture light and excite the space.
Photo: Andrew Bordwin
Design: William Sofield

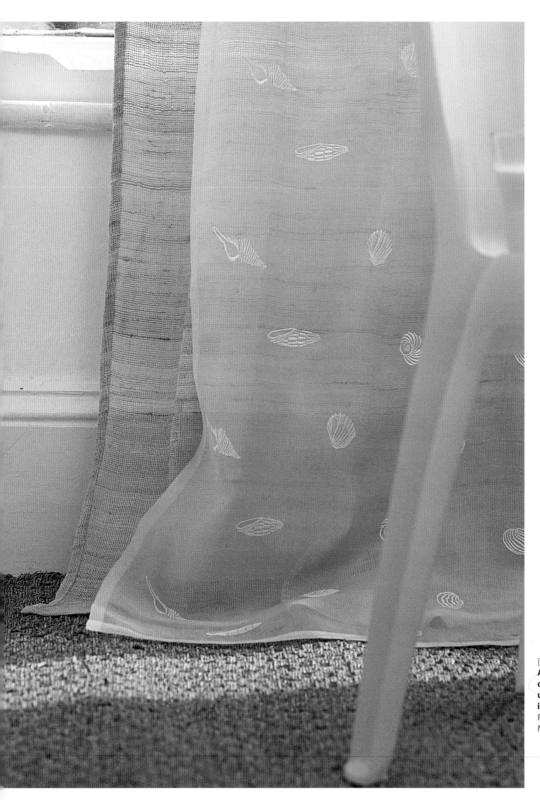

A simple treatment to create an outdoor feel includes jute carpet underfoot. Add double sheer drapery in natural tones and airy fabric.
Photo: L. Pope, courtesy of IPC Magazines Ltd.

SEE COLOR IN ITS TRUE LIGHT

Colors appear different in different light. Ambient light is affected by the surfaces that reflect that light. Keying your palette to your surroundings, then, takes advantage of the natural light by making your interior more luminescent and cohesive. Oceanfront homes suggest a palette in the blue and green range, whereas a desert home might call for neutrals in earthy or sandy tones.

[ABOVE]

Natural fibers create an aura of the outdoors, even if used only in accent pieces. Raffia, unbleached cotton, linen, rattan, and reed add fresh air to your interior.

Photo: Courtesy of Zimmer and Rohde

CHOOSE TEXTURES INSPIRED BY NATURE

Let nature inspire textural choices to give a neutral decor an earthy feel. Imitate grainy sand in nubby upholstery fabrics. Paint walls with a colorwash to mimic the effect of slate or limestone.

Choose wood furnishings for their color and texture. A bamboo side table is not only lighter in tone than a polished mahogany piece but its texture also gives the room a lighter feeling.

[ABOVE]
Create a restful bedroom, natural style. A soft blend of cotton matelassé, linen, and sisal soften the look of exposed beams while complementing their natural feel.
Photo: Billy Cunningham
Design: Lisa Walker

[OPPOSITE]
A touch of greenery can dramatically change the feel of a room. A wispy potted fig makes a cozy reading corner feel like the outdoors.
Photo: Steve Vierra
Design: Diane Hughe

[ABOVE]
Fresh cotton fabrics and natural wood against a white backdrop give a room a fresh-air feel. Bamboo furnishings and large potted plants add the outdoor touch that completes the look.
Photo: E. Reeve, courtesy of IPC Magazines Ltd.

[OPPOSITE]
Let daylight fill your room through windows draped in sunny yellow. Hardwood floors and natural fabrics in neutral tones sit comfortably under a potted tree to turn a living room into an outdoor experience.
Photo: Courtesy of Zimmer and Rohde

[RIGHT]
A rustic look isn't the only way to bring nature into your home. Elegant polished wood and fine furnishings in neutral fabrics pick up the feeling from the streaming sunlight and the burnished autumn tones in the carpet and accent pillows.
Photo:
www.davidduncanlivingston.com

analogous colors
colors that appear side-by-side on the color wheel

art deco
a style of architecture and furnishings popular in the 1920s and 1930s; characteristics include streamlined, geometric motifs expressed in materials such as glass, plastic, and chrome

batiste
a fine, plain-woven fabric

bedskirt
fabric attached to a bed below the mattress and draping to the floor. Can be gathered, pleated, or flat. Also called a dust ruffle

brocade
fabric with extra threads woven into it to create elaborate, raised designs (or) a heavy textile with a raised design resembling embroidery

brushed (cotton)
a fabric with a nap produced by brushing

calico
a coarse, plain weave cotton, usually brightly printed

challis
a light fabric of wool, cotton, or rayon

chenille
a fabric made of a soft tufted silk, cotton or worsted cord or yarn

chintz
a firm, usually glazed cotton fabric of plain weave often with colorful printed designs

colorwash
a painting technique whereby a mix of glaze and paint is applied over a base coat to create rich, multi-toned effect

combing
a painting technique whereby a comb is dragged across a wet base coat or glaze to create a wood-grained effect

complementary colors
colors that appear opposite one another on the color wheel

cool colors
colors on the color wheel from blue-violet through green; they make an object appear to be farther away or a room bigger than it really is

cut velvet
velvet with patterns cut into the pile

damask
traditionally made of silk, this fabric now made from cotton, linen, or wool. With cotton, the richly figurative design is produced by the contrast of a sateen and satin woven crosswise against each other

dhurrie
a traditional, colorful Indian woven carpet, usually made of cotton or silk

duck
a durable, closely woven heavy cotton or linen fabric

duvet
a quilt, usually with a washable cover, used in place of a bedspread and top sheet

feng shui
the ancient Chinese art of placement, which incorporates many Eastern beliefs into a practice that is said to enhance the well-being of the inhabitants of a home through adjustments to the use of color and the placement of furnishings and objects

gingham
a fine, yet firm cotton cloth with stripes running in both directions, creating a regular checked effect

gray
to lessen the intensity of a color by adding its complement

hue
color of the spectrum

ikat
fabric that is dip-dyed before weaving so that subtle patterns are created along the warp

inlay
a method of decorating the surface of furniture or flooring where cuts or grooves in the wood are filled with differently colored wood, mother-of-pearl, ceramic, or metal

intensity
brightness or dullness of a color

kilim
a reversible woven rug made in the Middle East or Central Asia, usually made of wool and displaying geometric designs

lace
a delicate, openwork fabric of intricate patterned design usually made from linen, cotton, silk, or metal threads

linen
cloth woven of threads made from the flax plant

moiré
a wavy design on silk or other fabrics that gives a watered appearance

monochromatic
a color scheme based on one color in various tones, shades, or textures

motif
a recurring architectural or decorative design

obelisk (-shaped tower)
a four-sided shape that tapers to a pyramidal point

ombre (or ombré)
fabrics dyed or woven in graduated color from light to dark

organza
a stiff, slightly starchy textured sheer fabric that is made from a twisted silk warp yarn

paisley
a woven or printed colorful, swirled pattern of abstract, curved shapes, derived from the palmette motif of Persian rugs

pile
the surface texture of carpet or fabric that stands upright

pillow sham
a removable decorative pillow cover

plissé
fabric with a puckered look

primary colors
red, blue, and yellow

rayon
a synthetic textile fiber produced by forcing a cellulose solution through fine spinnerets

rib
a raised ridge or wale in cloth or knitted material

secondary colors
mixes of equal parts of two primary colors

shade
to darken the value of a color by adding black

split complementary colors
colors whose positions on the color wheel form an equilateral triangle

sponging
a painting technique whereby colors are applied with a sponge over a base coat to create textured effect

stippling
a painting technique whereby a wet glaze coat (usually oil-based) is dabbed on with a dry brush to create a grainy texture

taffeta
a smooth, crisp fabric with a slight sheen

tapestry
a heavy cloth woven with rich, complex, often varicolored designer scenes

tertiary colors
mixes of equal parts of a primary and a secondary color

tint
to lighten the value of a color by adding white

toile
a sheer linen fabric or a heavy, colorfully printed, unglazed cotton, linen, or rayon fabric used for drapery or slipcovers (fine cretonne printed on a single color)

triads
colors whose positions on the color wheel form an equilateral triangle

value
darkness or lightness of a color

twill
a fabric with diagonal, parallel ribs

variegated
having streaks, marks, or patches of a different color or colors

velvet
a closely woven pile fabric, usually made of cotton or synthetic fiber, with two warp threads—one for the pile and one for the ground

velour
a closely napped, velvet-like fabric

voile
a sheer fabric used especially for making light dresses and curtains

warm colors
colors on the color wheel from yellow-green through violet; they make an object appear to be closer or a room smaller than it is

Wedgwood blue
the blue color typical of the trademark pottery made by Josiah Wedgwood and his successors

Glossary sources:

Carniger, Denise L. *The New Decorating Book.* Des Moines, Iowa: Better Homes and Gardens Books, 1997. pp. 404-5.

Gillat, Mary. *The Decorating Book.* New York: Pantheon Books, 1981. pp. 360-1.

Innes, Jocasta and Blake, Jill. *The Conran Beginner's Guide to Decorating.* London: Conran Octopus Limited, 1987. pp.184-7.

Paine, Melanie. *The New Fabric Magic.* New York: Pantheon Books, 1987. pp. 206-7.

Webster's *II New Collegiate Dictionary.* Boston: Houghton Mifflin Company, 1999.

ABC Carpet and Home
881 & 888 Broadway at East
19th Street
New York, NY 10003
212-473-3000
www.abchome.com

Anichini
Route 110
Turnbridge, VT 05077
800-553-5309
www.anichini.com

Anthropologie
1700 Sansom Street, 6th Floor
Philadelphia, PA 19103
800-309-2500 or 800-543-1039
www.anthropologie.com

Barclay Leaf Imports, Inc.
21 Wilson Terrace
Elizabeth, NJ 07208
908-353-9284 or 908-353-5525

Bed and Bath
12817 Preston Road, Suite 128
Dallas, TX 75230
800-945-7714 or 972-783-9502
www.bedandbath.com

Bed, Bath, and Beyond
800-GO-BEYOND
www.bedbathandbeyond.com

Crate & Barrel
800-967-6696
www.crateandbarrel.com

Donghia Furniture/Textiles Ltd.
International Headquarters
485 Broadway
New York, NY 10013-2607
Telephone: 212-925-2777
Fax: 212-925-4819
e-mail: DonghiaNY@aol.com

Essential Home
3775 24th Street
San Francisco, CA 94114
888-282-3330
www.essentialhome.com

Garnet Hill
800-622-6216
www.garnethill.com

IKEA
800-434-ikea
www.ikea.com

Lee Jofa
800-453-3563
www.leejofa.com

Linens 'n Things
6 Brighton Road
Clifton, NJ 07015
973-815-2974
www.linensnthings.com

Luminaire
301 West Superior
Chicago, IL 60610
800-494-4358

Marimekko Oyj
Puusepänkatu 4
00810 Helsinki Finland
Telephone: +358 9-75871
Fax: +358 9-7553051
www.marimekko.fi

Nono
Altrincham WA14 SDY
United Kingdom
Telephone: +44 1565 757 400
Fax: +44 1565 757 405
www.nono.co.uk

Pier 1 Imports
461 Fifth Ave
New York, NY 10017
800-447-4371
www.pier1.com

Pottery Barn
P.O. Box 7044
San Francisco, CA 94120
800-922-5507
www.potterybarn.com

Progress Paint, KCI
201 East Market Street
Louisville, KY 40202
502-584-0151

Sherwin-Williams Co.
www.sherwin-williams.com

Spiegel
P.O. Box 182555
Columbus, OH 43218-2555
800-474-5555
www.spiegel.com

Takashimaya
693 Fifth Avenue
New York, NY 10022
800-753-2038

The Conran Shop
Michelin House
81 Fulham Road
London SW3 6RD
+44 (0)171-591-8702
www.conran.co.uk

The Silk Trading Co.
800-854-0396
www.silktrading.com

Urban Archaeology
143 Franklin Street
New York, NY 10013
212-431-4646

Zimmer + Rohde
Zimmersmühlenweg 14-18
D-61440 Oberusel
Germany
Telephone: +49 617163202
Fax: +49 6171632244
http://www.zr-group.com

Adjaye and Russell
Architecture Design
24 Sunbury Workshops
Swanfield Street London E2 7LF
United Kingdom
Telephone: +44 171-739-4969
Fax: +44 171-739-3484
E-mail:
dadjaye@compuserve.com

Jacob D. Albert
Albert, Righter, Tittman
Architects, Inc.
58 Winter Street
Boston, MA 02108
Telephone: 617-451-15740
Fax: 617-451-2309

B & B Italia
150 East 58th Street
New York, NY 10155

Christian Badin
52, rue Bourgogne
Paris 75007 France

Jeffery Bilhuber
330 East 59th Street, 6th Floor
New York, NY 10022
Telephone: 212-308-4888
Fax: 212-223-4590
bilhuber@aol.com

Laura Bohn
c/o Michael Dunne
54 Stokenchurch Street
London SW6 3TR
United Kingdom
+44 171-736-617

MaryClare Brandt, ASID
MC Brandt Interior Design
P.O. Box 8276
La Jolla, CA 92037

Madeleine Castaing
21, rue Bonaparte
Paris 75006
France

Francois Catroux
20, rue du Faubourg Saint
Honoré
Paris 75008 France

Cha & Innerhofer
Architecture & Design
611 Broadway, Suite 540
New York, NY 10012
Telephone: 212-477-6957
Fax: 212-353-3286

Linda Chase Associates Inc.
482 Town Street
East Haddam, CT 06423
Telephone: 860-873-9499
Fax: 860-873-9496

James Edwin Choate
Surber Barber Choate &
Hertlein Architects
1389 Peachtree Street NE
Atlanta, GA 30309

Eric Caspers Ciborowski
85 bis, rue Billancourt
Boulogne 92000 France

Celeste Cooper
1415 Boylston Street
Boston, MA 02116
Telephone: 212-826-5667
Fax: 617-426-1879

Charles Correa
Architects/Planners
9 Mathew Road
Bombay 400 004 India
Telephone: +91 22-363-3307 or
22-364-5195
Fax: +91 22-363-1138

Yoggy Crow, Inc.
330 Oak Lane
Richmond, VA 23226
Telephone: 804-359-6429
Fax: 804-358-3985

Carden Cunietti Limited
83 Westbourne Park Road
London W2 5QH
United Kingdom
Telephone: +44 207-229-8559
Fax: +44 207-229-8799

Robert D'Ario
9, rue des Coffes
Toulouse 31000 France

Tony Duquette
1354 Dawnbridge Drive
Beverly Hills, CA 90202
310-271-3574

J. Frank Fitzgibbons
Associates
4822 Glencairn Road
Los Angeles, CA 90027

Frank Fitzpatrick
1637 Silver Lake Boulevard
Los Angeles, CA 90039

Berns Fry
Berns Fry Interiors
75 Swamp Road
East Hampton, NY 11937
631-725-8157

Michael Gabellini
Gabellini Associates Architects
665 Broadway
New York, NY 10012
212-388-1700

Eric Gizard
6, rue Jules Chaplin
Paris 75006 France

Marian Glasgow
9 Lowell Street
Newton Center, MA 02450
617-965-0936

Zina Glazabrook
Z.G. Designs
10 Wireless Road
East Hampton, NY 11937
519-329-7486

Phyllis G. Goldberg, ASID
PGG Interiors
P.O. Box 14427
East Providence, RI 02914
401-331-7077

Mark Guard Ltd Architects
161 Whitfield Street
London W1P 5RY
United Kingdom
Telephone: +44 171-380-1199
Fax: +44 171-387-5441

Michelle Halard
Yves Halard
252 bis, boulevard Saint
Germain
Paris 75007 France

Tangee Harris-Pritchett
Tangee Inc.
5306 South Hyde Park
Boulevard
Chicago, IL 60657
773-327-7101

Danny Hartley Interiors, Inc.
1653 North McFaraland
Boulevard
Tuscaloosa, AL 35406
Telephone: 205-345-9578
Fax: 205-345-9565

Hardy Holzman Pfeiffer Associates
902 Broadway
New York, NY 10010
Telephone: 212-677-6030
Fax: 212-979-1677

Kelly Hoppen Interiors
2 Alma Studios
32 Stratford Road
Kensington
London WB 6QF
United Kingdom
Telephone: +44 171-938-4151
Fax: +44 171-938-1878

Diane Hughes
Diane Hughes Interiors
29 Lafayette Road
North Hampton, NH 03862
603-964-9543

Malin Iovino Design
43 Saint Saviours Wharf
Mill Street
London W9 1RS
United Kingdom
Telephone: +44 171-252-3542
Fax: +44 171-252-3542

The Iron Shop
P.O. Box 547
400 Reed Road
Broomall, PA 19008

Fujiwo Ishimoto
Marimekko OYJ
Inf. Department
Puusepankatu 4
00810 Helsinki Finland

Kristina Isola
Marimekko OYJ
Inf. Department
Puusepankatu 4
00810 Helsinki Finland

Maija Isola
Marimekko OYJ
Inf. Department
Puusepankatu 4
00810 Helsinki Finland

Dakota Jackson, Inc.
42-24 Orchard Street, 5th Floor
Long Island City, NY 11101
718-786-8600

Charlotte S. Jensen, ASID
11464 Escoda Place
San Diego, CA 92127-1015

Richard Kazarian Antiques
11 Church Street
Providence, RI 02904
401-331-0079

Annie Kelly
2075 Watsonia Terrace
Los Angeles, CA 90068

Marc Klein
30 Sycamore Lane
Roslyn Heights, NY 11577

Scott Marble & Karen Fairbanks Architects
66 West Broadway, #600
New York, NY 10007
Telephone: 212-233-0653
Fax: 212-233-0654

Mark Mack Architects
246 First Street
San Francisco, CA 94103

Jeffery Alan Marks
7746 Herschel Avenue
La Jolla, CA 92037 and
1007 Montana Avenue
Santa Monica, CA 90403

Linda McCalla Interiors
604 South Church Street
Georgetown, TX 78626
Telephone: 512-930-9987
Fax: 512-869-0666

McDowell & Benedetti
62 Roseberry Avenue
London EC1R 4RR
United Kingdom
Telephone: +44 171-278-8810
Fax: +44 171-278-8844

Frederic Mechiche
4, rue Thorigny
Paris 75003 France

MMM Architects
The Banking Hall
28 Maida Vale
London W9 1RS
United Kingdom
Telephone: +44 207-286-9499
Fax: +44 207-286-9599
E-mail: post@mmm.demon.co.uk

Moutarde
Flat 8, 8-13 New Inn Street
London ECZ A 3PY
United Kingdom
+44 171-384-8789

Gill Nono
Nono Designs Craven Court
Altrincham WA14 SDY
United Kingdom
Telephone: +44 161-929-9930
Fax: +44 161-929-9951

Benjamin Noriega-Ortiz
75 Spring Street
New York, NY 10012
212-343-9709

Patrice Nourissat
230, rue des Pyrenees
Paris 75020 France

Thomas O'Brien
132 Spring Street
New York, NY 10012
Telephone: 212-966-4700
Fax: 212-966-4701

Ravage Cours des Fabriques
70, rue Jean-Pierre Timland
Paris France

Ruffle & Hook Interior
122-124 St. John Street
Clerkenwell
London EC1V 4JS
United Kingdom

William Sofield
Studio Sofield Inc.
380 Lafayette Street
New York, NY 1000
212-473-1300

Galia Solomonoff Projects
249 West 29th Street
New York, NY 10001
Telephone: 212-268-1569
Fax: 212-631-0379

Stamberg Aferiat Architecture
126 Fifth Avenue
New York, NY 10011

Stedila Design
135 East 55th Street
New York, NY 10022

Arlene Stone
c/o David Duncan Livingston
1036 Erica Road
Mill Valley, CA 94941
415-383-0898

Lisa Walker
P.O. Box 80526
Phoenix, AZ 85060
602-952-2908

Marshall Watson Interiors, Ltd.
105 West 72nd Street, 9B
New York, NY 10023

David Webster
254 West 25th Street
New York, NY 10001
212-924-8932

Weixler, Peterson & Luzi
2031 Locust Street
Philadelphia, PA 19103
215-854-0391

Vicente Wolf Associates, Inc.
333 West 39th Street
New York, NY 10018
Telephone: 212-465-0590
Fax: 212-465-0639

Dianna Wong
315 West 9th Street
Los Angeles, CA 90015

Mark Zeff
260 West 72nd Street,
Suite 12B
New York, NY 10023
212-580-7090

Zimmer and Rohde
Zimmersmühlenweg 14-18
D-61440 Oberursel
Germany
Telephone: 06171-632-146
Fax: 06171-632-244

Peter Aprahamian
30 Nelson Road
London N8 9RU
United Kingdom
+44 181 482 4840

Roland Beaufre Photography
53 rue du Faubourg Saint
Antoine
Paris 75011 France
Telephone: +33 1 53176394
Fax: +33 1 43409165

Andrew Bordwin Studios, Inc.
70A Greenwich Avenue
New York, NY 10011
Telephone: 212-627-9519
Fax: 212-924-1791

Grey Crawford Photography
2924 Park Center Drive
Los Angeles, CA 90068
Telephone: 213-413-4299
Fax: 323-851-4252

Billy Cunningham
140 Seventh Avenue, Apt. 4C
New York, NY 10011

Guillaume de Laubier
14 rue Victor Hugo
92000 Nanterre
France
+33 147-21-6645

Jacques Dirand
10 Passgae Doisy
Paris 75017 France
Telephone: +33 14574-11-64
Fax: +33 014068-99-95

Michael Dunne
54 Stokenchurch Street
London SW6 3TR
United Kingdom
+44 171-736-617

Pieter Estersohn Photography
c/o La Chapelle
Representation Ltd.
420 East 54th Street
New York, NY 10022
Telephone: 212-838-3170
Fax: 212-758-6199

Dan Forer
6815 Southwest 81st Terrace
Miami, FL 33143
Telephone: 305-667-3646
Fax: 305-667-4733

Bill Geddes
215 West 78th Street
New York, NY 10024
Telephone: 212-799-4464
Fax: 212-799-5576

Ed Gohlich
P.O. Box 180919
Coronado, CA 92178
619-423-4237

Marianne Haas
28 Stadelhoferstrasse
8001 Zurich
Switzerland
+41 1 261 0904

Paul Harmer
10 Hartland Road
London NW6 6BJ
United Kingdom

Alec Hemer
81 Bedford Street, #5E
New York, NY 10014

Eduard Hueber
Eduard Hueber Arch Photo,
Inc.
51 White Street
New York, NY 10013
Telephone: 212-941-9294
Fax: 212-941-9317

IPC Magazines, Ltd.
King's Reach Tower
Stamford Street
London SE1 9LS
United Kingdom

IKEA
800-434-ikea
www.ikea.com

David Joseph Snaps
523 Broadway, #5
New York, NY 10012
Telephone: 212-226-3535
Fax: 212-334-9155

David Duncan Livingston
1036 Erica Road
Mill Valley, CA 94941
415-383-0898
www.davidduncanlivingston.com

Richard S. Mandelkorn
RSM Photography
65 Beaver Pond Road
Lincoln, MA 01773
Telephone: 781-259-3310
Fax: 781-259-3312

Peter Margonelli
20 Desbrosses Street
New York, NY 10013
212-941-0380

Marimekko
Marimekko OYJ
Inf. Department
Puusepankatu 4
00810 Helsinki Finland

Norman McGrath Photography
164 West 79th Street
New York, NY 10024
212-799-6422

**Matthew Millman
Photography**
3127 Eton Avenue
Berkeley, CA 94705
510-459-9030

Eric Morin
7 rue de Bourgogne
75007 Paris France

Michael Mundy
Michael Mundy Photography Inc.
25 Mercer Street, #3B
New York, NY 10013
Telephone: 212-226-4741
Fax: 212-343-2936

Sam Ogden
273 Summer Street
Boston, MA 02210
Telephone: 617-426-1021
Fax: 617-426-1021

Dorothy Perry
2124 North Whipple Avenue
Chicago, IL 60647
773-278-5446

David Phelps
6305 Yucca Street, #601
Los Angeles, CA 90001
Telephone: 323-464-7297
Fax: 323-464-7238

Ed Reeve
Pickwick Studio
Ebenezer Street
London N1 7NP
United Kingdom

Laura Rensen
422 West Broadway, #3
New York, NY 10012
212-334-1862

Kenneth Rice Photography
456 Sixty-first Street
Oakland, CA 94509
Telephone: 510-652-1752
Fax: 510-658-4355

Eric Roth Studio
P.O. Box 422
Topsfield, MA 01983
978-887-1975

Bill Rothschild
19 Judith Lane
Wesley Hills, NY 10952
212-752-3674

Rion Rizzo
Creative Sources Photography
6095 Lake Forrest Drive, #100
Atlanta, GA 30328

Tim Street-Porter
2074 Watsonia Terrace
Los Angeles CA 90068
323-874-4278

Tim Soar
62 Roseberry Avenue
London EC1R 4RR
United Kingdom
+44 171 278 8810

Steve Vierra Photography
P.O. Box 1827
Sandwich, MA 02563
508-477-7043

Andreas von Einsiedel
72-80 Leather Lane
London EC1N 7TR
United Kingdom

Richard Waite
16 Powis Mews
London W11 1JN
United Kingdom
Telephone: +44 171-229-6919
Fax: +44 171-229-3446

William Waldron Photography
27 Bleeker Street, 6A
New York, NY 10012

Paul Warchol Photography
224 Centre Street
New York, NY 10013
Telephone: 212-431-3461
Fax: 212-274-1953

Henry Wilson
The Interior Archive Ltd
15 Grand Union Centre, West
Row
London W10 5AS
United Kingdom
Telephone: +44 171-370-0595
Fax: +44 181-960-2695

Patrick Y. Wong
Atelier Wong Photography
1009 E. 40th Street, Suite 100
Austin, TX 78751
512-371-1288

Toshi Yoshimi Photography
4030 Camero Ave
Los Angeles, CA 90027
Telephone: 323-660-9043
Fax: 323-660-2497

**Elizabeth Zeschin
Photography**
Studio 6, The Old Library
125 Battersea High Street
London SE11 3HY
United Kingdom

Ann McArdle is a freelance writer who lives and works in Gloucester, Massachusetts. Recently retired from a career in publishing, she writes on a wide range of topics.

Her books on interior design include the series *Minimal Interiors*, *Romantic Interiors*, *Elegant Interiors*, *Natural Interiors*, and *Harmonious Interiors*, and *East-West Style*, all published by Rockport Publishers. Another book, *Stephanie's Angels*, a human interest story, is published by Twin Lights Publishers.

In her free time, McArdle studies yoga and tutors at Gloucester's Wellspring House, Inc. in their Foundations Program teaching career skills to women in transition.